PREGNANCY

Journal and Planner for Special Things to Come!

Date

how do i feel?

Weight :

Waist Measurement :

- [ ] higher ♥ rate?
- [ ] emotional?
- [ ] warmer hands&feet?
- [ ] acne?
- [ ] increased thirst
- [ ] veins more noticeable in breast?

sickness :

cravings :

milestone :

Things to do :

- [ ]
- [ ]
- [ ]
- [ ]
- [ ]
- [ ]
- [ ]
- [ ]
- [ ]
- [ ]
- [ ]
- [ ]

Next check-up schedule :

Supplements :

Preparations for Baby :

how do i feel?

Date

Weight :

Waist Measurement :

- [ ] higher ♥ rate?
- [ ] emotional?
- [ ] warmer hands&feet?
- [ ] acne?
- [ ] increased thirst
- [ ] veins more noticeable in breast?

sickness :

cravings :

milestone :

Things to do :

- [ ]
- [ ]
- [ ]
- [ ]
- [ ]
- [ ]
- [ ]
- [ ]
- [ ]
- [ ]
- [ ]
- [ ]

Next check-up schedule :

Supplements :

Preparations for Baby :

Date

how do i feel? ____________

Weight : ____________

Waist Measurement : ____________

- [ ] higher ♥ rate?
- [ ] emotional?
- [ ] warmer hands&feet?
- [ ] acne?
- [ ] increased thirst
- [ ] veins more noticeable in breast?

sickness : ____________

milestone :

cravings : ____________

Things to do :

- [ ] ____________
- [ ] ____________
- [ ] ____________
- [ ] ____________
- [ ] ____________
- [ ] ____________
- [ ] ____________
- [ ] ____________
- [ ] ____________
- [ ] ____________
- [ ] ____________
- [ ] ____________

Next check-up schedule :

Supplements :

Preparations for Baby :

how do i feel? ____________

Date ____________

Weight : ____________

Waist Measurement : ____________

- [ ] higher ♥ rate?
- [ ] emotional?
- [ ] warmer hands&feet?
- [ ] acne?
- [ ] increased thirst
- [ ] veins more noticeable in breast?

sickness : ____________

cravings : ____________

milestone :

Things to do :

- [ ] ____________
- [ ] ____________
- [ ] ____________
- [ ] ____________
- [ ] ____________
- [ ] ____________
- [ ] ____________
- [ ] ____________
- [ ] ____________
- [ ] ____________
- [ ] ____________
- [ ] ____________

Next check-up schedule :

Supplements :

Preparations for Baby :

photo
here

Date

how do i feel? ____________

____

____

____

Weight : ____________

Waist Measurement : ____________

- [ ] higher ♥ rate?
- [ ] emotional?
- [ ] warmer hands&feet?
- [ ] acne?
- [ ] increased thirst
- [ ] veins more noticeable in breast?

sickness : ____________

cravings : ____________

milestone :

Things to do :

- [ ] ____________
- [ ] ____________
- [ ] ____________
- [ ] ____________
- [ ] ____________
- [ ] ____________
- [ ] ____________
- [ ] ____________
- [ ] ____________
- [ ] ____________
- [ ] ____________
- [ ] ____________

Next check-up schedule :

Supplements :

Preparations for Baby :

how do i feel? ____________

Date ____________

Weight : ____________

Waist Measurement : ____________

- [ ] higher ♥ rate?
- [ ] emotional?
- [ ] warmer hands&feet?
- [ ] acne?
- [ ] increased thirst
- [ ] veins more noticeable in breast?

sickness : ____________

cravings : ____________

milestone :

Things to do :

- [ ] ____________
- [ ] ____________
- [ ] ____________
- [ ] ____________
- [ ] ____________
- [ ] ____________
- [ ] ____________
- [ ] ____________
- [ ] ____________
- [ ] ____________
- [ ] ____________
- [ ] ____________

Next check-up schedule :

Supplements :

Preparations for Baby :

Date

how do i feel?

Weight :

Waist Measurement :

- [ ] higher ♥ rate?
- [ ] emotional?
- [ ] warmer hands&feet?
- [ ] acne?
- [ ] increased thirst
- [ ] veins more noticeable in breast?

sickness :

milestone :

cravings :

Things to do :

- [ ]
- [ ]
- [ ]
- [ ]
- [ ]
- [ ]
- [ ]
- [ ]
- [ ]
- [ ]
- [ ]
- [ ]

Next check-up schedule :

Supplements :

Preparations for Baby :

Date

how do i feel?

Weight :

Waist Measurement :

- [ ] higher ♥ rate?
- [ ] emotional?
- [ ] warmer hands&feet?
- [ ] acne?
- [ ] increased thirst
- [ ] veins more noticeable in breast?

sickness :

cravings :

milestone :

Things to do :

- [ ]
- [ ]
- [ ]
- [ ]
- [ ]
- [ ]
- [ ]
- [ ]
- [ ]
- [ ]
- [ ]
- [ ]

Next check-up schedule :

Supplements :

Preparations for Baby :

photo
here

Date

how do i feel?

Weight :

Waist Measurement :

- [ ] higher ♥ rate?
- [ ] emotional?
- [ ] warmer hands&feet?
- [ ] acne?
- [ ] increased thirst
- [ ] veins more noticeable in breast?

sickness :

cravings :

milestone :

Things to do :

- [ ]
- [ ]
- [ ]
- [ ]
- [ ]
- [ ]
- [ ]
- [ ]
- [ ]
- [ ]
- [ ]
- [ ]

Next check-up schedule :

Supplements :

Preparations for Baby :

how do i feel? ____________

____

____

____

Date ____________

Weight : ____________

Waist Measurement : ____________

- [ ] higher ♥ rate?
- [ ] emotional?
- [ ] warmer hands&feet?
- [ ] acne?
- [ ] increased thirst
- [ ] veins more noticeable in breast?

sickness : ______________

cravings : ______________

milestone :

Things to do :

- [ ] ______________
- [ ] ______________
- [ ] ______________
- [ ] ______________
- [ ] ______________
- [ ] ______________
- [ ] ______________
- [ ] ______________
- [ ] ______________
- [ ] ______________
- [ ] ______________
- [ ] ______________

Next check-up schedule :

Supplements :

Preparations for Baby :

how do i feel? ____________

____

____

____

Date ____________

Weight : ____________

Waist Measurement : ____________

- [ ] higher ♥ rate?
- [ ] emotional?
- [ ] warmer hands&feet?
- [ ] acne?
- [ ] increased thirst
- [ ] veins more noticeable in breast?

sickness : ____________

cravings : ____________

milestone :

Things to do :

- [ ] ____________
- [ ] ____________
- [ ] ____________
- [ ] ____________
- [ ] ____________
- [ ] ____________
- [ ] ____________
- [ ] ____________
- [ ] ____________
- [ ] ____________
- [ ] ____________
- [ ] ____________

Next check-up schedule :

Supplements :

Preparations for Baby :

how do i feel? ____________

____

____

____

Date ____________

Weight : ____________

Waist Measurement : ____________

- [ ] higher ♥ rate?
- [ ] emotional?
- [ ] warmer hands&feet?
- [ ] acne?
- [ ] increased thirst
- [ ] veins more noticeable in breast?

sickness : ____________

cravings : ____________

milestone :

Things to do :

- [ ] ____________
- [ ] ____________
- [ ] ____________
- [ ] ____________
- [ ] ____________
- [ ] ____________
- [ ] ____________
- [ ] ____________
- [ ] ____________
- [ ] ____________
- [ ] ____________
- [ ] ____________

Next check-up schedule :

Supplements :

Preparations for Baby :

photo
here

how do i feel? ____________

____

____

____

Date ____________

Weight : ____________

Waist Measurement : ____________

- [ ] higher ♥ rate?
- [ ] emotional?
- [ ] warmer hands&feet?
- [ ] acne?
- [ ] increased thirst
- [ ] veins more noticeable in breast?

sickness : ____________

cravings : ____________

milestone :

Things to do :

- [ ] ____________
- [ ] ____________
- [ ] ____________
- [ ] ____________
- [ ] ____________
- [ ] ____________
- [ ] ____________
- [ ] ____________
- [ ] ____________
- [ ] ____________
- [ ] ____________
- [ ] ____________

Next check-up schedule :

Supplements :

Preparations for Baby :

Date

how do i feel?

Weight :

Waist Measurement :

- [ ] higher ♥ rate?
- [ ] emotional?
- [ ] warmer hands&feet?
- [ ] acne?
- [ ] increased thirst
- [ ] veins more noticeable in breast?

sickness :

cravings :

milestone :

Things to do :

- [ ]
- [ ]
- [ ]
- [ ]
- [ ]
- [ ]
- [ ]
- [ ]
- [ ]
- [ ]
- [ ]
- [ ]

Next check-up schedule :

Supplements :

Preparations for Baby :

Date

how do i feel? ___________

Weight : ___________

Waist Measurement : ___________

- [ ] higher ♥ rate?
- [ ] emotional?
- [ ] warmer hands&feet?
- [ ] acne?
- [ ] increased thirst
- [ ] veins more noticeable in breast?

sickness : ___________

milestone :

cravings : ___________

Things to do :

- [ ] ___________
- [ ] ___________
- [ ] ___________
- [ ] ___________
- [ ] ___________
- [ ] ___________
- [ ] ___________
- [ ] ___________
- [ ] ___________
- [ ] ___________
- [ ] ___________
- [ ] ___________

Next check-up schedule :

Supplements :

Preparations for Baby :

Date

how do i feel?

Weight :

Waist Measurement :

- [ ] higher ♥ rate?
- [ ] emotional?
- [ ] warmer hands&feet?
- [ ] acne?
- [ ] increased thirst
- [ ] veins more noticeable in breast?

sickness :

cravings :

milestone :

Things to do :

- [ ]
- [ ]
- [ ]
- [ ]
- [ ]
- [ ]
- [ ]
- [ ]
- [ ]
- [ ]
- [ ]
- [ ]

Next check-up schedule :

Supplements :

Preparations for Baby :

photo
here

how do i feel?

Date

Weight :

Waist Measurement :

- [ ] higher ♥ rate?
- [ ] emotional?
- [ ] warmer hands&feet?
- [ ] acne?
- [ ] increased thirst
- [ ] veins more noticeable in breast?

sickness :

cravings :

milestone :

Things to do :

- [ ]
- [ ]
- [ ]
- [ ]
- [ ]
- [ ]
- [ ]
- [ ]
- [ ]
- [ ]
- [ ]
- [ ]

Next check-up schedule :

Supplements :

Preparations for Baby :

Date

how do i feel?

Weight :

Waist Measurement :

- ☐ higher ♥ rate?
- ☐ emotional?
- ☐ warmer hands&feet?
- ☐ acne?
- ☐ increased thirst
- ☐ veins more noticeable in breast?

sickness :

cravings :

milestone :

Things to do :

- ☐
- ☐
- ☐
- ☐
- ☐
- ☐
- ☐
- ☐
- ☐
- ☐
- ☐
- ☐

Next check-up schedule :

Supplements :

Preparations for Baby :

how do i feel? ____________

Date ____________

Weight : ____________

Waist Measurement : ____________

- [ ] higher ♥ rate?
- [ ] emotional?
- [ ] warmer hands&feet?
- [ ] acne?
- [ ] increased thirst
- [ ] veins more noticeable in breast?

sickness : ____________

cravings : ____________

milestone :

Things to do :

- [ ] ____________
- [ ] ____________
- [ ] ____________
- [ ] ____________
- [ ] ____________
- [ ] ____________
- [ ] ____________
- [ ] ____________
- [ ] ____________
- [ ] ____________
- [ ] ____________
- [ ] ____________

Next check-up schedule :

Supplements :

Preparations for Baby :

how do i feel?

Date

Weight :

Waist Measurement :

- [ ] higher ♥ rate?
- [ ] emotional?
- [ ] warmer hands&feet?
- [ ] acne?
- [ ] increased thirst
- [ ] veins more noticeable in breast?

sickness :

milestone :

cravings :

Things to do :

- [ ]
- [ ]
- [ ]
- [ ]
- [ ]
- [ ]
- [ ]
- [ ]
- [ ]
- [ ]
- [ ]
- [ ]

Next check-up schedule :

Supplements :

Preparations for Baby :

photo
here

Date

how do i feel?

Weight :

Waist Measurement :

- [ ] higher ♥ rate?
- [ ] emotional?
- [ ] warmer hands&feet?
- [ ] acne?
- [ ] increased thirst
- [ ] veins more noticeable in breast?

sickness :

cravings :

milestone :

Things to do :

- [ ]
- [ ]
- [ ]
- [ ]
- [ ]
- [ ]
- [ ]
- [ ]
- [ ]
- [ ]
- [ ]
- [ ]

Next check-up schedule :

Supplements :

Preparations for Baby :

how do i feel? ___________

Date

Weight : ___________

Waist Measurement : ___________

- [ ] higher ♥ rate?
- [ ] emotional?
- [ ] warmer hands&feet?
- [ ] acne?
- [ ] increased thirst
- [ ] veins more noticeable in breast?

sickness : ___________

milestone :

cravings : ___________

Things to do :

- [ ] ___________
- [ ] ___________
- [ ] ___________
- [ ] ___________
- [ ] ___________
- [ ] ___________
- [ ] ___________
- [ ] ___________
- [ ] ___________
- [ ] ___________
- [ ] ___________
- [ ] ___________

Next check-up schedule :

Supplements :

Preparations for Baby :

how do i feel? ___________

Date

Weight : ___________

Waist Measurement : ___________

- [ ] higher ♥ rate?
- [ ] emotional?
- [ ] warmer hands&feet?
- [ ] acne?
- [ ] increased thirst
- [ ] veins more noticeable in breast?

sickness : ___________

cravings : ___________

milestone :

Things to do :

- [ ]
- [ ]
- [ ]
- [ ]
- [ ]
- [ ]
- [ ]
- [ ]
- [ ]
- [ ]
- [ ]
- [ ]

Next check-up schedule :

Supplements :

Preparations for Baby :

how do i feel? ___________

Date ___________

Weight : ___________

Waist Measurement : ___________

- [ ] higher ♥ rate?
- [ ] emotional?
- [ ] warmer hands&feet?
- [ ] acne?
- [ ] increased thirst
- [ ] veins more noticeable in breast?

sickness : ___________

cravings : ___________

milestone :

Things to do :

- [ ] ___________
- [ ] ___________
- [ ] ___________
- [ ] ___________
- [ ] ___________
- [ ] ___________
- [ ] ___________
- [ ] ___________
- [ ] ___________
- [ ] ___________
- [ ] ___________
- [ ] ___________

Next check-up schedule :

Supplements :

Preparations for Baby :

photo
here

Date

how do i feel? ____________

____

____

____

Weight : ____________

Waist Measurement : ____________

- [ ] higher ♥ rate?
- [ ] emotional?
- [ ] warmer hands&feet?
- [ ] acne?
- [ ] increased thirst
- [ ] veins more noticeable in breast?

sickness : ________________

milestone :

cravings : ________________

Things to do :

- [ ] ________________
- [ ] ________________
- [ ] ________________
- [ ] ________________
- [ ] ________________
- [ ] ________________
- [ ] ________________
- [ ] ________________
- [ ] ________________
- [ ] ________________
- [ ] ________________
- [ ] ________________

Next check-up schedule :

Supplements :

Preparations for Baby :

how do i feel? ____________

____

____

____

Date ____________

Weight : ____________

Waist Measurement : ____________

- [ ] higher ♥ rate?
- [ ] emotional?
- [ ] warmer hands&feet?
- [ ] acne?
- [ ] increased thirst
- [ ] veins more noticeable in breast?

sickness : ____________

cravings : ____________

milestone :

Things to do :

- [ ] ____________
- [ ] ____________
- [ ] ____________
- [ ] ____________
- [ ] ____________
- [ ] ____________
- [ ] ____________
- [ ] ____________
- [ ] ____________
- [ ] ____________
- [ ] ____________
- [ ] ____________

Next check-up schedule :

Supplements :

Preparations for Baby :

how do i feel? ____________

Date ____________

Weight : ____________

Waist Measurement : ____________

- [ ] higher ♥ rate?
- [ ] emotional?
- [ ] warmer hands&feet?
- [ ] acne?
- [ ] increased thirst
- [ ] veins more noticeable in breast?

sickness : ____________

milestone :

cravings : ____________

Things to do :

- [ ] ____________
- [ ] ____________
- [ ] ____________
- [ ] ____________
- [ ] ____________
- [ ] ____________
- [ ] ____________
- [ ] ____________
- [ ] ____________
- [ ] ____________
- [ ] ____________
- [ ] ____________

Next check-up schedule :

Supplements :

Preparations for Baby :

how do i feel? ___________

Date ___________

Weight : ___________

Waist Measurement : ___________

- [ ] higher ♥ rate?
- [ ] emotional?
- [ ] warmer hands&feet?
- [ ] acne?
- [ ] increased thirst
- [ ] veins more noticeable in breast?

sickness : ___________

cravings : ___________

milestone :

Things to do :

- [ ] ___________
- [ ] ___________
- [ ] ___________
- [ ] ___________
- [ ] ___________
- [ ] ___________
- [ ] ___________
- [ ] ___________
- [ ] ___________
- [ ] ___________
- [ ] ___________
- [ ] ___________

Next check-up schedule :

Supplements :

Preparations for Baby :

photo
here

Date

how do i feel? ____________

Weight : ____________

Waist Measurement : ____________

- [ ] higher ♥ rate?
- [ ] emotional?
- [ ] warmer hands&feet?
- [ ] acne?
- [ ] increased thirst
- [ ] veins more noticeable in breast?

sickness : ____________

milestone :

cravings : ____________

Things to do :

- [ ] ____________
- [ ] ____________
- [ ] ____________
- [ ] ____________
- [ ] ____________
- [ ] ____________
- [ ] ____________
- [ ] ____________
- [ ] ____________
- [ ] ____________
- [ ] ____________
- [ ] ____________

Next check-up schedule :

Supplements :

Preparations for Baby :

how do i feel? ____________

____

____

____

Date ____________

Weight : ____________

Waist Measurement : ____________

- [ ] higher ♥ rate?
- [ ] emotional?
- [ ] warmer hands&feet?
- [ ] acne?
- [ ] increased thirst
- [ ] veins more noticeable in breast?

sickness : ____________

cravings : ____________

milestone :

Things to do :

- [ ] ____________
- [ ] ____________
- [ ] ____________
- [ ] ____________
- [ ] ____________
- [ ] ____________
- [ ] ____________
- [ ] ____________
- [ ] ____________
- [ ] ____________
- [ ] ____________
- [ ] ____________

Next check-up schedule :

Supplements :

Preparations for Baby :

Date

how do i feel? ____________

Weight : ____________

Waist Measurement : ____________

- [ ] higher ♥ rate?
- [ ] emotional?
- [ ] warmer hands&feet?
- [ ] acne?
- [ ] increased thirst
- [ ] veins more noticeable in breast?

sickness : ____________

cravings : ____________

milestone :

Things to do :

- [ ] ____________
- [ ] ____________
- [ ] ____________
- [ ] ____________
- [ ] ____________
- [ ] ____________
- [ ] ____________
- [ ] ____________
- [ ] ____________
- [ ] ____________
- [ ] ____________
- [ ] ____________

Next check-up schedule :

Supplements :

Preparations for Baby :

how do i feel? ____________

____

____

____

Date ____________

Weight : ____________

Waist Measurement : ____________

- [ ] higher ♥ rate?
- [ ] emotional?
- [ ] warmer hands&feet?
- [ ] acne?
- [ ] increased thirst
- [ ] veins more noticeable in breast?

sickness : ________________

cravings : ________________

milestone :

Things to do :

- [ ] ________________
- [ ] ________________
- [ ] ________________
- [ ] ________________
- [ ] ________________
- [ ] ________________
- [ ] ________________
- [ ] ________________
- [ ] ________________
- [ ] ________________
- [ ] ________________
- [ ] ________________

Next check-up schedule :

Supplements :

Preparations for Baby :

photo
here

Date

how do i feel? ____________

Weight : ____________

Waist Measurement : ____________

- [ ] higher ♥ rate?
- [ ] emotional?
- [ ] warmer hands&feet?
- [ ] acne?
- [ ] increased thirst
- [ ] veins more noticeable in breast?

sickness : ____________

cravings : ____________

milestone :

Things to do :

- [ ] ____________
- [ ] ____________
- [ ] ____________
- [ ] ____________
- [ ] ____________
- [ ] ____________
- [ ] ____________
- [ ] ____________
- [ ] ____________
- [ ] ____________
- [ ] ____________
- [ ] ____________

Next check-up schedule :

Supplements :

Preparations for Baby :

how do i feel? ____________

____

____

____

Date

Weight : __________

Waist Measurement : ________

- [ ] higher ♥ rate?
- [ ] emotional?
- [ ] warmer hands&feet?
- [ ] acne?
- [ ] increased thirst
- [ ] veins more noticeable in breast?

sickness : ________________

milestone :

cravings : ________________

Things to do :

- [ ] ________________
- [ ] ________________
- [ ] ________________
- [ ] ________________
- [ ] ________________
- [ ] ________________
- [ ] ________________
- [ ] ________________
- [ ] ________________
- [ ] ________________
- [ ] ________________
- [ ] ________________

Next check-up schedule :

Supplements :

Preparations for Baby :

Date

how do i feel? ___________

____

____

____

Weight : ___________

Waist Measurement : ___________

- [ ] higher ♥ rate?
- [ ] emotional?
- [ ] warmer hands&feet?
- [ ] acne?
- [ ] increased thirst
- [ ] veins more noticeable in breast?

sickness : ___________

cravings : ___________

milestone :

Things to do :

- [ ] ___________
- [ ] ___________
- [ ] ___________
- [ ] ___________
- [ ] ___________
- [ ] ___________
- [ ] ___________
- [ ] ___________
- [ ] ___________
- [ ] ___________
- [ ] ___________
- [ ] ___________

Next check-up schedule :

Supplements :

Preparations for Baby :

how do i feel? ____________

Date

Weight : ____________

Waist Measurement : ____________

- [ ] higher ♥ rate?
- [ ] emotional?
- [ ] warmer hands&feet?
- [ ] acne?
- [ ] increased thirst
- [ ] veins more noticeable in breast?

sickness : ____________

milestone :

cravings : ____________

Things to do :

- [ ]
- [ ]
- [ ]
- [ ]
- [ ]
- [ ]
- [ ]
- [ ]
- [ ]
- [ ]
- [ ]
- [ ]

Next check-up schedule :

Supplements :

Preparations for Baby :

photo
here

how do i feel? ___________

Date ___________

Weight : ___________

Waist Measurement : ___________

- [ ] higher ♥ rate?
- [ ] emotional?
- [ ] warmer hands&feet?
- [ ] acne?
- [ ] increased thirst
- [ ] veins more noticeable in breast?

sickness : ___________

milestone :

cravings : ___________

Things to do :

- [ ] ___________
- [ ] ___________
- [ ] ___________
- [ ] ___________
- [ ] ___________
- [ ] ___________
- [ ] ___________
- [ ] ___________
- [ ] ___________
- [ ] ___________
- [ ] ___________
- [ ] ___________

Next check-up schedule :

Supplements :

Preparations for Baby :

how do i feel? ___________

Date

Weight : ___________

Waist Measurement : ___________

- [ ] higher ♥ rate?
- [ ] emotional?
- [ ] warmer hands&feet?
- [ ] acne?
- [ ] increased thirst
- [ ] veins more noticeable in breast?

sickness : ___________

milestone :

cravings : ___________

Things to do :

- [ ] ___________
- [ ] ___________
- [ ] ___________
- [ ] ___________
- [ ] ___________
- [ ] ___________
- [ ] ___________
- [ ] ___________
- [ ] ___________
- [ ] ___________
- [ ] ___________
- [ ] ___________

Next check-up schedule :

Supplements :

Preparations for Baby :

Date

how do i feel? ___________

____

____

____

Weight : __________

Waist Measurement : __________

- [ ] higher ♥ rate?
- [ ] emotional?
- [ ] warmer hands&feet?
- [ ] acne?
- [ ] increased thirst
- [ ] veins more noticeable in breast?

sickness : ______________

cravings : ______________

milestone :

Things to do :

- [ ] ______________
- [ ] ______________
- [ ] ______________
- [ ] ______________
- [ ] ______________
- [ ] ______________
- [ ] ______________
- [ ] ______________
- [ ] ______________
- [ ] ______________
- [ ] ______________
- [ ] ______________

Next check-up schedule :

Supplements :

Preparations for Baby :

how do i feel? ____________

Date

Weight : ____________

Waist Measurement : ____________

- [ ] higher ♥ rate?
- [ ] emotional?
- [ ] warmer hands&feet?
- [ ] acne?
- [ ] increased thirst
- [ ] veins more noticeable in breast?

sickness : ____________

milestone :

cravings : ____________

Things to do :

- [ ] ____________
- [ ] ____________
- [ ] ____________
- [ ] ____________
- [ ] ____________
- [ ] ____________
- [ ] ____________
- [ ] ____________
- [ ] ____________
- [ ] ____________
- [ ] ____________
- [ ] ____________

Next check-up schedule :

Supplements :

Preparations for Baby :

photo
here

Date

how do i feel?

Weight :

Waist Measurement :

- [ ] higher ♥ rate?
- [ ] emotional?
- [ ] warmer hands&feet?
- [ ] acne?
- [ ] increased thirst
- [ ] veins more noticeable in breast?

sickness :

milestone :

cravings :

Things to do :

- [ ]
- [ ]
- [ ]
- [ ]
- [ ]
- [ ]
- [ ]
- [ ]
- [ ]
- [ ]
- [ ]
- [ ]

Next check-up schedule :

Supplements :

Preparations for Baby :

how do i feel? ____________

Date ____________

Weight : ____________

Waist Measurement : ____________

- [ ] higher ♥ rate?
- [ ] emotional?
- [ ] warmer hands&feet?
- [ ] acne?
- [ ] increased thirst
- [ ] veins more noticeable in breast?

sickness : ____________

cravings : ____________

milestone :

Things to do :

- [ ] ____________
- [ ] ____________
- [ ] ____________
- [ ] ____________
- [ ] ____________
- [ ] ____________
- [ ] ____________
- [ ] ____________
- [ ] ____________
- [ ] ____________
- [ ] ____________
- [ ] ____________

Next check-up schedule :

Supplements :

Preparations for Baby :

Date

how do i feel? ___________

____

____

____

Weight : ___________

Waist Measurement : ________

- [ ] higher ♥ rate?
- [ ] emotional?
- [ ] warmer hands&feet?
- [ ] acne?
- [ ] increased thirst
- [ ] veins more noticeable in breast?

sickness : _______________

milestone :

cravings : _______________

Things to do :

- [ ] ______________
- [ ] ______________
- [ ] ______________
- [ ] ______________
- [ ] ______________
- [ ] ______________
- [ ] ______________
- [ ] ______________
- [ ] ______________
- [ ] ______________
- [ ] ______________
- [ ] ______________

Next check-up schedule :

Supplements :

Preparations for Baby :

how do i feel? ____________

Date

Weight : ________

Waist Measurement : ________

- [ ] higher ♥ rate?
- [ ] emotional?
- [ ] warmer hands&feet?
- [ ] acne?
- [ ] increased thirst
- [ ] veins more noticeable in breast?

sickness : ____________

milestone :

cravings : ____________

Things to do :

- [ ] ____________
- [ ] ____________
- [ ] ____________
- [ ] ____________
- [ ] ____________
- [ ] ____________
- [ ] ____________
- [ ] ____________
- [ ] ____________
- [ ] ____________
- [ ] ____________
- [ ] ____________

Next check-up schedule :

Supplements :

Preparations for Baby :

photo
here

Date

how do i feel? ___________

Weight : ___________

Waist Measurement : ___________

- [ ] higher ♥ rate?
- [ ] emotional?
- [ ] warmer hands&feet?
- [ ] acne?
- [ ] increased thirst
- [ ] veins more noticeable in breast?

sickness : ___________

cravings : ___________

milestone :

Things to do :

- [ ] ___________
- [ ] ___________
- [ ] ___________
- [ ] ___________
- [ ] ___________
- [ ] ___________
- [ ] ___________
- [ ] ___________
- [ ] ___________
- [ ] ___________
- [ ] ___________
- [ ] ___________

Next check-up schedule :

Supplements :

Preparations for Baby :

how do i feel? ____________

Date

Weight : ____________

Waist Measurement : ____________

- [ ] higher ♥ rate?
- [ ] emotional?
- [ ] warmer hands&feet?
- [ ] acne?
- [ ] increased thirst
- [ ] veins more noticeable in breast?

sickness : ____________

cravings : ____________

milestone :

Things to do :

- [ ] ____________
- [ ] ____________
- [ ] ____________
- [ ] ____________
- [ ] ____________
- [ ] ____________
- [ ] ____________
- [ ] ____________
- [ ] ____________
- [ ] ____________
- [ ] ____________
- [ ] ____________

Next check-up schedule :

Supplements :

Preparations for Baby :

Date

how do i feel? ____________

Weight : ____________

Waist Measurement : ____________

- [ ] higher ♥ rate?
- [ ] emotional?
- [ ] warmer hands&feet?
- [ ] acne?
- [ ] increased thirst
- [ ] veins more noticeable in breast?

sickness : ____________

milestone :

cravings : ____________

Things to do :

- [ ] ____________
- [ ] ____________
- [ ] ____________
- [ ] ____________
- [ ] ____________
- [ ] ____________
- [ ] ____________
- [ ] ____________
- [ ] ____________
- [ ] ____________
- [ ] ____________
- [ ] ____________

Next check-up schedule :

Supplements :

Preparations for Baby :

Date

how do i feel?

Weight :

Waist Measurement :

- [ ] higher ♥ rate?
- [ ] emotional?
- [ ] warmer hands&feet?
- [ ] acne?
- [ ] increased thirst
- [ ] veins more noticeable in breast?

sickness :

cravings :

milestone :

Things to do :

- [ ]
- [ ]
- [ ]
- [ ]
- [ ]
- [ ]
- [ ]
- [ ]
- [ ]
- [ ]
- [ ]
- [ ]

Next check-up schedule :

Supplements :

Preparations for Baby :

photo
here

how do i feel?

Date

Weight :

Waist Measurement :

- [ ] higher ♥ rate?
- [ ] emotional?
- [ ] warmer hands&feet?
- [ ] acne?
- [ ] increased thirst
- [ ] veins more noticeable in breast?

sickness :

cravings :

milestone :

Things to do :

- [ ]
- [ ]
- [ ]
- [ ]
- [ ]
- [ ]
- [ ]
- [ ]
- [ ]
- [ ]
- [ ]
- [ ]

Next check-up schedule :

Supplements :

Preparations for Baby :

how do i feel?

Date

Weight :

Waist Measurement :

- [ ] higher ♥ rate?
- [ ] emotional?
- [ ] warmer hands&feet?
- [ ] acne?
- [ ] increased thirst
- [ ] veins more noticeable in breast?

sickness :

milestone :

cravings :

Things to do :

- [ ]
- [ ]
- [ ]
- [ ]
- [ ]
- [ ]
- [ ]
- [ ]
- [ ]
- [ ]
- [ ]
- [ ]

Next check-up schedule :

Supplements :

Preparations for Baby :

how do i feel? ___________

Date ___________

Weight : ___________

Waist Measurement : ___________

- [ ] higher ♥ rate?
- [ ] emotional?
- [ ] warmer hands&feet?
- [ ] acne?
- [ ] increased thirst
- [ ] veins more noticeable in breast?

sickness : ___________

milestone :

cravings : ___________

Things to do :

- [ ] ___________
- [ ] ___________
- [ ] ___________
- [ ] ___________
- [ ] ___________
- [ ] ___________
- [ ] ___________
- [ ] ___________
- [ ] ___________
- [ ] ___________
- [ ] ___________
- [ ] ___________

Next check-up schedule :

Supplements :

Preparations for Baby :

how do i feel? ____________

Date

Weight : ____________

Waist Measurement : ____________

- [ ] higher ♥ rate?
- [ ] emotional?
- [ ] warmer hands&feet?
- [ ] acne?
- [ ] increased thirst
- [ ] veins more noticeable in breast?

sickness : ____________

milestone :

cravings : ____________

Things to do :

- [ ] ____________
- [ ] ____________
- [ ] ____________
- [ ] ____________
- [ ] ____________
- [ ] ____________
- [ ] ____________
- [ ] ____________
- [ ] ____________
- [ ] ____________
- [ ] ____________
- [ ] ____________

Next check-up schedule :

Supplements :

Preparations for Baby :

photo
here

how do i feel? ___________

Date ___________

Weight : ___________

Waist Measurement : ___________

- [ ] higher ♥ rate?
- [ ] emotional?
- [ ] warmer hands&feet?
- [ ] acne?
- [ ] increased thirst
- [ ] veins more noticeable in breast?

sickness : ___________

cravings : ___________

milestone :

Things to do :

- [ ] ___________
- [ ] ___________
- [ ] ___________
- [ ] ___________
- [ ] ___________
- [ ] ___________
- [ ] ___________
- [ ] ___________
- [ ] ___________
- [ ] ___________
- [ ] ___________
- [ ] ___________

Next check-up schedule :

Supplements :

Preparations for Baby :

Date

how do i feel? ____________

____

____

____

Weight : __________

Waist Measurement : ________

- [ ] higher ♥ rate?
- [ ] emotional?
- [ ] warmer hands&feet?
- [ ] acne?
- [ ] increased thirst
- [ ] veins more noticeable in breast?

sickness : ______________

cravings : ______________

milestone :

Things to do :

- [ ] ______________
- [ ] ______________
- [ ] ______________
- [ ] ______________
- [ ] ______________
- [ ] ______________
- [ ] ______________
- [ ] ______________
- [ ] ______________
- [ ] ______________
- [ ] ______________
- [ ] ______________

Next check-up schedule :

Supplements :

Preparations for Baby :

how do i feel? ____________

____
____
____

____
Date

Weight : ____________

Waist Measurement : __________

- [ ] higher ♥ rate?
- [ ] emotional?
- [ ] warmer hands&feet?
- [ ] acne?
- [ ] increased thirst
- [ ] veins more noticeable in breast?

sickness : __________________

cravings : __________________

milestone :

Things to do :

- [ ] ________________
- [ ] ________________
- [ ] ________________
- [ ] ________________
- [ ] ________________
- [ ] ________________
- [ ] ________________
- [ ] ________________
- [ ] ________________
- [ ] ________________
- [ ] ________________
- [ ] ________________

Next check-up schedule :

Supplements :

Preparations for Baby :

how do i feel? ____________

Date ____________

Weight : ____________

Waist Measurement : ____________

- [ ] higher ♥ rate?
- [ ] emotional?
- [ ] warmer hands&feet?
- [ ] acne?
- [ ] increased thirst
- [ ] veins more noticeable in breast?

sickness : ____________

milestone :

cravings : ____________

Things to do :

- [ ] ____________
- [ ] ____________
- [ ] ____________
- [ ] ____________
- [ ] ____________
- [ ] ____________
- [ ] ____________
- [ ] ____________
- [ ] ____________
- [ ] ____________
- [ ] ____________
- [ ] ____________

Next check-up schedule :

Supplements :

Preparations for Baby :

photo
here

Date

how do i feel?

Weight :

Waist Measurement :

- [ ] higher ♥ rate?
- [ ] emotional?
- [ ] warmer hands&feet?
- [ ] acne?
- [ ] increased thirst
- [ ] veins more noticeable in breast?

sickness :

cravings :

milestone :

Things to do :

- [ ]
- [ ]
- [ ]
- [ ]
- [ ]
- [ ]
- [ ]
- [ ]
- [ ]
- [ ]
- [ ]
- [ ]

Next check-up schedule :

Supplements :

Preparations for Baby :

how do i feel? ___________

Date

Weight : ___________

Waist Measurement : ___________

- [ ] higher ♥ rate?
- [ ] emotional?
- [ ] warmer hands&feet?
- [ ] acne?
- [ ] increased thirst
- [ ] veins more noticeable in breast?

sickness : ___________

milestone :

cravings : ___________

Things to do :

- [ ]
- [ ]
- [ ]
- [ ]
- [ ]
- [ ]
- [ ]
- [ ]
- [ ]
- [ ]
- [ ]
- [ ]

Next check-up schedule :

Supplements :

Preparations for Baby :

how do i feel? ____________

Date ____________

Weight : ____________

Waist Measurement : ____________

- ☐ higher ♥ rate?
- ☐ emotional?
- ☐ warmer hands&feet?
- ☐ acne?
- ☐ increased thirst
- ☐ veins more noticeable in breast?

sickness : ____________

cravings : ____________

milestone :

Things to do :

- ☐ ____________
- ☐ ____________
- ☐ ____________
- ☐ ____________
- ☐ ____________
- ☐ ____________
- ☐ ____________
- ☐ ____________
- ☐ ____________
- ☐ ____________
- ☐ ____________
- ☐ ____________

Next check-up schedule :

Supplements :

Preparations for Baby :

how do i feel?

Date

Weight :

Waist Measurement :

- [ ] higher ♥ rate?
- [ ] emotional?
- [ ] warmer hands&feet?
- [ ] acne?
- [ ] increased thirst
- [ ] veins more noticeable in breast?

sickness :

milestone :

cravings :

Things to do :

- [ ]
- [ ]
- [ ]
- [ ]
- [ ]
- [ ]
- [ ]
- [ ]
- [ ]
- [ ]
- [ ]
- [ ]

Next check-up schedule :

Supplements :

Preparations for Baby :

photo
here

Date

how do i feel? ____________

____

____

____

Weight : ____________

Waist Measurement : ____________

- [ ] higher ♥ rate?
- [ ] emotional?
- [ ] warmer hands&feet?
- [ ] acne?
- [ ] increased thirst
- [ ] veins more noticeable in breast?

sickness : ____________

milestone :

cravings : ____________

Things to do :

- [ ] ____________
- [ ] ____________
- [ ] ____________
- [ ] ____________
- [ ] ____________
- [ ] ____________
- [ ] ____________
- [ ] ____________
- [ ] ____________
- [ ] ____________
- [ ] ____________
- [ ] ____________

Next check-up schedule :

Supplements :

Preparations for Baby :

how do i feel? ____________

Date

Weight : ____________

Waist Measurement : ____________

- [ ] higher ♥ rate?
- [ ] emotional?
- [ ] warmer hands&feet?
- [ ] acne?
- [ ] increased thirst
- [ ] veins more noticeable in breast?

sickness : ____________

cravings : ____________

milestone :

Things to do :

- [ ]
- [ ]
- [ ]
- [ ]
- [ ]
- [ ]
- [ ]
- [ ]
- [ ]
- [ ]
- [ ]
- [ ]

Next check-up schedule :

Supplements :

Preparations for Baby :

how do i feel? ___________

Date ___________

Weight : ___________

Waist Measurement : ___________

☐ higher ♥ rate?
☐ emotional?
☐ warmer hands&feet?
☐ acne?
☐ increased thirst
☐ veins more noticeable in breast?

sickness : ___________

milestone :

cravings : ___________

Things to do :

☐ ___________
☐ ___________
☐ ___________
☐ ___________
☐ ___________
☐ ___________
☐ ___________
☐ ___________
☐ ___________
☐ ___________
☐ ___________
☐ ___________

Next check-up schedule :

Supplements :

Preparations for Baby :

how do i feel? ___________

____

____

____

Date ___________

Weight : ___________

Waist Measurement : ___________

- [ ] higher ♥ rate?
- [ ] emotional?
- [ ] warmer hands&feet?
- [ ] acne?
- [ ] increased thirst
- [ ] veins more noticeable in breast?

sickness : ___________

cravings : ___________

milestone :

Things to do :

- [ ] ___________
- [ ] ___________
- [ ] ___________
- [ ] ___________
- [ ] ___________
- [ ] ___________
- [ ] ___________
- [ ] ___________
- [ ] ___________
- [ ] ___________
- [ ] ___________
- [ ] ___________

Next check-up schedule :

Supplements :

Preparations for Baby :

photo
here

how do i feel? ____________

____

____

____

Date ____________

Weight : ____________

Waist Measurement : ____________

- [ ] higher ♥ rate?
- [ ] emotional?
- [ ] warmer hands&feet?
- [ ] acne?
- [ ] increased thirst
- [ ] veins more noticeable in breast?

sickness : ____________

cravings : ____________

milestone :

Things to do :

- [ ] ____________
- [ ] ____________
- [ ] ____________
- [ ] ____________
- [ ] ____________
- [ ] ____________
- [ ] ____________
- [ ] ____________
- [ ] ____________
- [ ] ____________
- [ ] ____________
- [ ] ____________

Next check-up schedule :

Supplements :

Preparations for Baby :

how do i feel? ____________

Date

Weight : ________

Waist Measurement : ________

- [ ] higher ♥ rate?
- [ ] emotional?
- [ ] warmer hands&feet?
- [ ] acne?
- [ ] increased thirst
- [ ] veins more noticeable in breast?

sickness : ____________

cravings : ____________

milestone :

Things to do :

- [ ] ____________
- [ ] ____________
- [ ] ____________
- [ ] ____________
- [ ] ____________
- [ ] ____________
- [ ] ____________
- [ ] ____________
- [ ] ____________
- [ ] ____________
- [ ] ____________
- [ ] ____________

Next check-up schedule :

Supplements :

Preparations for Baby :

how do i feel? ___________

Date ___________

Weight : ___________

Waist Measurement : ___________

- [ ] higher ♥ rate?
- [ ] emotional?
- [ ] warmer hands&feet?
- [ ] acne?
- [ ] increased thirst
- [ ] veins more noticeable in breast?

sickness : ___________

milestone :

cravings : ___________

Things to do :

- [ ] ___________
- [ ] ___________
- [ ] ___________
- [ ] ___________
- [ ] ___________
- [ ] ___________
- [ ] ___________
- [ ] ___________
- [ ] ___________
- [ ] ___________
- [ ] ___________
- [ ] ___________

Next check-up schedule :

Supplements :

Preparations for Baby :

how do i feel? ____________

Date

Weight : __________

Waist Measurement : ________

- [ ] higher ♥ rate?
- [ ] emotional?
- [ ] warmer hands&feet?
- [ ] acne?
- [ ] increased thirst
- [ ] veins more noticeable in breast?

sickness : ______________

milestone :

cravings : ______________

Things to do :

- [ ]
- [ ]
- [ ]
- [ ]
- [ ]
- [ ]
- [ ]
- [ ]
- [ ]
- [ ]
- [ ]
- [ ]

Next check-up schedule :

Supplements :

Preparations for Baby :

photo
here

www.ingramcontent.com/pod-product-compliance
Lightning Source LLC
LaVergne TN
LVHW080848170826
845678LV00006B/1748

* 9 7 9 8 8 6 9 4 4 4 3 7 0 *